D1525389

Beverly Hills

Beverly Hills Shield

Beverly Hills 1-Day Tour

By Clare Auchterlonie

Address:

Unanchor Press
P.O. Box 184
Durham, NC 27701
www.unanchor.com

Ordering Information:

Quantity sales. Special discounts are available on quantity purchases by corporations, associations, and others. For details, contact the publisher at the address above.

Orders by U.S. trade bookstores and wholesalers. Please contact Unanchor at hello@unanchor.com, or visit http://www.unanchor.com.

Printed in the United States of America

Unanchor is a global family for travellers to experience the world with the heart of a local.

UNANCHOR

Table of Contents

Introduction

=============

Do you want to be treated like a Pretty Woman or be arrested by the sight of a Beverly Hills Cop? If so, then this tour of Beverly Hills is just the one for you. The city of the very rich and ridiculously famous is just 5.7 square miles but has the most infamous zip code on the planet - 90210.

The biggest A-List celebrities live (or have lived) in Beverly Hills but the wonders of Beverly Hills can be enjoyed by anyone - not just the multi-millionaires that live there.

Whatever your budget in this one day, part driving but mostly walking tour of Beverly Hills, you'll get to see where Los Angeles rich and famous dine and shop!

So slip into the Jimmy Choo's of a 'Real Housewife' and experience a day in the life of Beverly Hills. From the frivolous to the ridiculous, this Beverly Hills tour will show you the ins and outs of the real Beverly Hills.

You can walk down the fabled Rodeo Drive and shop in such luxury stores as Chanel, Gucci, Louis Vuitton, Bulgari, Christian Dior, Versace and Tiffany. You'll be able to pop in to Cartier or Harry Winston to see the fabulous jewels worn by Oscar nominated stars as they walk the red carpet at The Academy Awards.

You will see the legendary Regency Beverly Wilshire Hotel at the end of Rodeo, where Richard Gere and Julia Roberts fell in love.

And at the end of this tour and you can dine like a star for the night - and maybe even spot a few famous faces - book a reservation at any one of these celebrity-friendly restaurants - Spago, Mr Chow, or The Polo Lounge at the Beverly Hills hotel.

So whether you are a glamorous wannabe or just curious how the other side lives, this tour is full of Beverly Hills' treasures for the first time Los Angeles visitor or someone wanting to go a bit deeper into this world famous district.

Included:

- Budget friendly itinerary with the opportunity to splurge for those who want to indulge.
- Pictures and maps of locations to help guide you around without a smartphone.
- General tips about visiting Los Angeles from a local.
- Off the beaten path suggestions from a local.
- Suggestions on other ways to save money on your trip.
- Lunch and dinner suggestions for every budget.
- Pictures and maps of locations to help guide you around without a smartphone.
- Tour can be easily swapped around for your convenience.

Day 1

=============

9:00 am -- The Fountain Coffee Room at The Beverly Hills Hotel

- Price: $20.00 (for a single adult)
- Duration: 1 hour
- Address: 9641 Sunset Boulevard, Beverly Hills 90210

It's hard to believe that the world famous city of Beverly Hills was once nothing more than a bunch of Lima bean fields. After speculators gave up on finding oil within what would become the Beverly Hills city limits, they found water and decided to develop the bean fields into housing. By 1911, developers were still having trouble selling the lots and it's then that they came up with the idea to market Beverly Hills as a resort and at the center would be a grand hotel with bungalows for guests with families. And so the Beverly Hills Hotel was built, born and opened in 1912. It seems fitting that your tour starts here.

Rooms go for anywhere from $550 a night in the main hotel to $1500+ a night for a Bungalow and upwards of $15,000 a night for one of the two new presidential bungalows, which opened in 2011.

You may not be able to afford to stay here but breakfast in the **Fountain Coffee Room** is an affordable way to visit this historic and beautiful hotel. Parking is $8 with validation. But, if you don't mind walking, then find street parking and walk up. Whether you plump for parking or not, you will start your day off right with breakfast at the **Beverly Hills Hotel.**

Enter the hotel and head right, past the front desk and follow the sign downstairs to the Fountain Room coffee shop. It's small with just seating for 19 at the counter. If there are more than 2 of you, you may have a wait, especially on weekends.

Is it worth it? Well, it amazes me that they get something as simple as eggs and hash browns so good! Whilst they use only the freshest ingredients, we are pretty sure they use clarified butter to cook it in. Yum. You can check out the menu on their web site before going to get an idea of the cost. It's not cheap but it's not horrific either, two eggs any style plus coffee and tip should set you back about $25 pp.

Historical hotels have historic stories and the **Beverly Hills Hotel** has more than most. Eccentric billionaire Howard Hughes lived in one of group of the bungalows for almost 30 years at a cost of $350,000. He also left his Cadillac parked next to the hotel for two years, so the tires went flat and plants began growing in and out of it. Unsurprisingly, the Beverly Hills PD never gave him a ticket! In one year, he spent an estimated $11 million at the hotel. Elizabeth Taylor's father ran an art gallery in the Hotel lobby when she was a child, and she ended up honeymooning here six times! When she was with Richard Burton they liked to stay in Bungalow 5 and had a standing room service order for two bottles of vodka at breakfast, and two more at lunch. Not surprisingly, they'd get in huge fights during which plates and glasses would fly. It was here they drowned their sorrows after Burton lost the Oscar to John Wayne for his performance in True Grit. Legend goes that Wayne turned up at the Bungalow 5 after party and thrust his Oscar at Burton saying: 'You son of a bitch, you should have this, not me.' Madonna and Mariah Carey have also stayed at this 4-bedroom bungalow, which features a pool, specially put in at the request of publishing magnate Walter Annenberg; Sidney Poitier danced barefoot in the lobby after winning an Oscar for Lilies of the Field; Elton John had his 55th birthday party here. Although Marilyn Monroe spent more time in Bungalow 1, it was number 7 that was her favorite and therefore known as the Norma Jean. The hotel has always been happy to accommodate the whims of its guests and Marlene Dietrich had a 7-by-8-foot bed specially made for Bungalow 10, which is the same Bungalow that John Lennon and Yoko Ono hid out in for a week. Bungalows 14-21 are known as Bachelor's Row and past residents include Warren Beatty and Orson Welles.

The hotel also contains a famous restaurant **The Polo Lounge**. Rumor has it that it is named so because movie Cowboy and Beverly Hills Honoree Mayor Will Rogers and his movie star friends used to play weekend polo games at Rogers' ranch and after the games, the group would cool off at the hotel lounge. The scene of countless movie deals and power lunches, this is where President Nixon's chief of staff, H.R. Haldeman, and domestic affairs counselor John Enrlichman were having breakfast when they learned about the Watergate burglary in 1972. Hotel phone records ended up being key to the case that toppled Nixon's presidency and sent many of his aides to prison.

Enjoy a leisurely breakfast at the **Fountain Coffee Shop** counter, with first class service. Remembering that this was the very counter that Marilyn Monroe used to sip milkshakes at and where their manager signed Guns 'n' Roses. John Lennon & Yoko Ono, Howard Hughes, and Desi Arnaz also have hung out here.

Be sure to take a discrete wander around the public areas of the hotel on the same level as the coffee shop - the gift shop etc, take a peek at the pool that Katherine Hepburn used to jump in fully clothed in her tennis outfit and that Fred Astaire, who enjoyed reading showbiz newspapers by. Just around the side from the coffee shop near the entrance to the gym is a great photographic display of sporting occasions at the hotel.

Website: www.dorchestercollection.com

10:00 am -- Travel to Rodeo Drive

- Price: FREE
- Duration: 10 minutes

If you are not driving then ride sharing services like Uber or Lyft can take you from the Beverly Hills Hotel to the next destination. Unfortunately there's no public transport that takes this route. It's a short 10 min drive. You could also walk it, it's a rather nice walk along tree lined streets and you can admire the big houses, but it will take about 25 minutes.

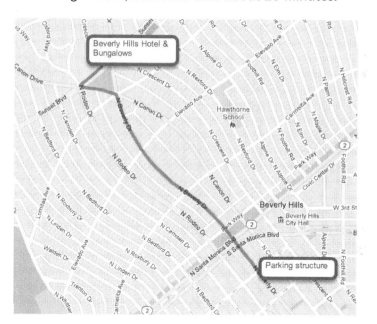

Turn right out of the Beverly Hills hotel, and head southwest on Sunset Blvd. Turn left onto Canon Drive, then right onto Beverly Drive. Take this over Santa Monica Blvd, and park in the city parking lot on the right. Free parking for two hours.

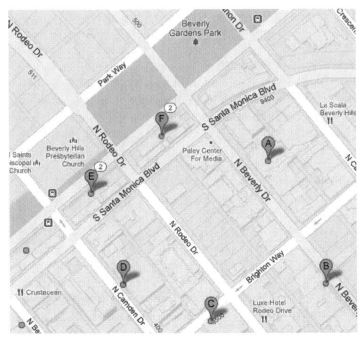

If that lot is full, you can try any of the public parking lots marked on the map above. For more details on public parking and rates in Beverly Hills see website: www.beverlyhills.org

10:10 am -- Walk to Beverly Hills Sign

- Price: FREE
- Duration: 5 minutes

Walk north up Beverly Drive towards Santa Monica Blvd. Cross over the road and turn right into Beverly Gardens Park.

10:15 am -- Beverly Hills Sign

- **Price:** FREE
- **Duration:** 15 minutes
- **Address:** North Santa Monica Blvd and North Beverly Drive, Beverly Hills, 90210

Situated in Beverly Gardens Park, which opened in 1911, the 40ft **Beverly Hills sign** is one of the most photographed spots in the city and is a fun way to start your visit so take a snap of you and the sign! The park is unusual in that it's narrow and long - 1.9 miles to be exact. From here to your left you can see the Beverly Hills City Hall and the Beverly Hills police station. The City Hall stood in for the police station in the movie Beverly Hills Cop in case you were wondering!

10:30 am -- Walk to Rodeo Drive

- Price: FREE
- Duration: 5 minutes

Head southwest (left if you are facing the sign) on Santa Monica Blvd towards Beverly Drive, turn left onto Rodeo Drive.

10:35 am -- Rodeo Drive

- Price: FREE
- Duration: 5 minutes
- Address: Rodeo Drive, Beverly Hills, 90210

Andy Warhol once said, *"Rodeo Drive is like a butterscotch sundae — even the nuts are delicious!"*

Probably the most expensive and famous shopping area in the world - **Rodeo Drive** (Roe-day-oh) is where celebrities and the very rich do their shopping, and where tourists window shop while trying to spot a celeb to gawk at. Rodeo Drive is a relatively small area - just three blocks known as the Golden Triangle - presumably, after the color Amex, you need to shop here! The Golden Triangle brings in around $20 Billion revenue a year.

As you walk down the left-hand side of the road you will pass Brook Bros, the first store on your left. Brooks Bros the oldest clothing company in the US (since 1818) President Lincoln is buried in one of their suits. Just past there at 440 is Dr Lancer - celebrity dermatologist - Oprah, Kim Kardashian, Ellen DeGeneres, Ryan Seacrest, Beyonce, Victoria Beckham have all been clients. Keep walking down till you get to the yellow building, often you will see a yellow Rolls-Royce parked outside.

10:40 am -- Bijan - the most expensive store in the world

- Price: FREE
- **Duration:** 5 minutes
- **Address:** 420 N Rodeo Drive, Beverly Hills, 90210

The most expensive store in the world, **Bijan**, named after its owner Bijan Pakzad, an Iranian-American designer. The names of some of Mr. Bijan's well-known clients are engraved on the front window of the boutique and an appointment is the only way to gain access into this exclusive world, where a pair of socks will cost you $100. A suit? $50,000. President Barack Obama, President George W. Bush, President Ronald Reagan, Russian President Vladimir Putin, Arnold Schwarzenegger, Tom

Cruise, the richest man in the world Carlos Slim Helu, designers Oscar Dela Renta, Tom Ford and Giorgio Armani and others who were keen to look good and had the money to foot the bill.

In 1981, Bijan created the first perfume for men and a 6 oz. bottle will set you back around $3,000. The Bijan perfume bottle is a featured exhibit at the Smithsonian.

The two-level $12 million store is the picture of opulence with Persian rugs, living trees that sprout from the floor, crystal chandeliers and Italian antiques. Sadly, there is no way you can go in and gawk at a $1000 tie as it's by appointment only and rumor has it in order just to get an appointment you need to make at least $1,000,000 a month.

You can take a virtual tour online or peek through the windows - note the chandelier in the main salon, its crystals are made of $1 million worth of Bijan perfume bottles (filled with real perfume!).

Website: www.bijan.com

As you walk to the next destination after you cross over Brighton Way and pass the Luxe Hotel, you will see an odd white building set back slightly from the road - this is **Anderton Court Shops** the last building completed by legendary American architect **Frank Lloyd Wright** in 1952.

10:45 am -- Harry Winston

- **Price:** FREE
- **Duration:** 5 minutes
- **Address:** 310 North Rodeo Drive, Beverly Hills, 90210

Known as the 'King of Diamonds', **Harry Winston** is one of the most famous jewelers' salons in the world. This is one of just eight Harry Winston jewelry salons in the US. After his death in 1978, the company is now run by his son Ronald who established the companies practice of lending jewelry to celebrities for events like the Oscars and Golden Globes. It's estimated that they lend over $200 million in diamonds to celebrities every year!

Harry Winston is also famous for supplying celebrity engagement rings including the rare 6 carat pink diamond that Ben Affleck gave Jennifer Lopez when they were dating. Ben bought his engagement ring for Jennifer Garner here as well. One of the most famous rings designed by Harry Winston is the iconic 69.42 carat diamond Richard Burton bought for Elizabeth Taylor which she later sold after they divorced for one of her charities for a cool $5 million! With prices starting at $10,000 Harry Winston diamond jewelry is definitely for a select market but there is no price on window shopping!

10:50 am -- Walk to Two Rodeo

- Price: FREE
- Duration: 5 minutes

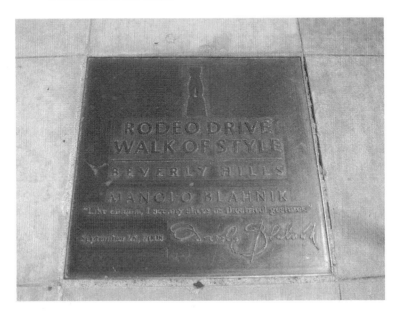

As you walk to Two Rodeo you will pass the **Rodeo Drive Walk of Style**. In 2003, Rodeo Drive Committee and the City of Beverly Hills, not wanting to be outdone by Hollywood, decided they wanted their own walk of fame to honor style legends for their contributions to the world of fashion. Recipients of the Rodeo Drive Walk of Style award include Giorgio Armani, Tom Ford, and Manolo Blahnik. See website for special events, etc: www.rodeodrive-bh.com

In the median, you will probably recognize one of Beverly Hills most recognizable bodies - an aluminum Torso statue by Robert Graham in 2003.

10:55 am -- Two Rodeo

- Price: FREE
- Duration: 15 minutes
- Address: 9480 Dayton Way #200, Beverly Hills, 90210

Two Rodeo Drive, with its small European cobblestone Disneyesque feel, is almost like a movie set - in fact it has been the backdrop for many fashion shoots, starred in TV shows like Entourage, and movies like Hollywood Homicide. It cost $2 million to build.

Despite its glamorous location, **Two Rodeo** is essentially a mall and the shops at Two Rodeo include Versace, Tiffany & Co., and Jimmy Choo. Food wise there is the world-renowned, and uber-pricey Japanese sushi house **Urasawa** where the average bill is said to come in around $1000, which is probably why it's the second most expensive restaurant in America!

There are two iconic places to get your picture taken here. The corner Via Rodeo and N. Rodeo Drive with the famous Rodeo street sign and the steps by Wilshire and the Fountain, so you can let all your friends back home know that you came, you saw... and at the least you took a picture!

11:10 am -- Walk to Beverly Wilshire Hotel

- **Price:** FREE
- **Duration:** 5 minutes

Walk up the cobbled streets of Two Rodeo and follow the road around and down the stairs. Across the street in front of you is the Beverly Wilshire Hotel.

11:15 am -- Beverly Wilshire Hotel

- Price: FREE
- Duration: 5 minutes
- Address: 9500 Wilshire Blvd, Beverly Hills, 90210

The uniquely E-shaped **Beverly Wilshire** has played host to many famous guests but it is best known for its role in the movie Pretty Woman. Richard Gere brings his new 'friend' Julia Robert here where they stay for 2 weeks, although at that time it was known as the Regent Beverly. Built in 1928, other long-term celebrity guests include Warren Beatty who lived in the penthouse suite, Elvis Presley who lived at the hotel during the 1950s for several years while making movies at the nearby Paramount Studios.

John Lennon stayed here for several months during the 70s while he was briefly estranged from Yoko. Other celebrities who have made the hotel their home for extended periods of time include Elton John, Mick Jagger, Andrew Lloyd Webber, and Cary Grant.

A night here will cost you $695 including breakfast but it does get you access to some celeb-worthy perks: car service within a three-mile radius; coffee, tea and mini pastries in the lobby; and chilled towels and frozen fruit at the hotel pool, as well as complimentary "sunglass-cleaning service." Alternatively how about The Pretty Woman Experience starting at $15,000?

Take a discreet wander through the lobby, while you won't see any Pretty Woman memorabilia there, there's an impressive $35,000 chandelier made of Swarovski crystals - it weighs over 700 lbs!

11:20 am -- Walk to Mr Chow

- Price: FREE
- Duration: 5 minutes

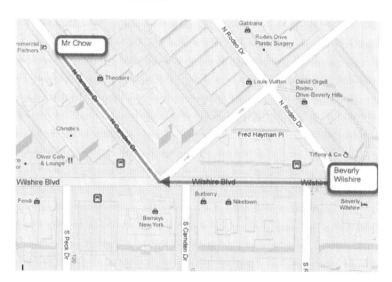

Walk west on Wilshire Blvd (right as you face the Beverly Wilshire from Rodeo), past Barneys New York (where Winona Ryder got caught shoplifting) and turn right up N Camden Drive. You will see **Mr Chow** half way up on the right hand side of the road.

11:25 am -- Mr Chow

- Price: FREE
- Duration: 5 minutes
- Address: 344 North Camden Drive, Beverly Hills, 90210

Michael Chow opened the first **Mr Chow** in Knightsbridge, London in 1968 at the height of Beatlemania. The Beatles, Jackie O and Marlene Dietrich were among its regular clientele. Due to the success of the London restaurant, this Beverly Hills location soon followed in 1974.

Since it first opened its doors, it's been one of the places to be seen and almost 40 years later celebrities are still regularly photographed leaving Mr Chow's. Serving expensive western style Chinese food, Mr Chow's is known by locals as a place to be seen and to people watch than to actually eat. Spot the paparazzo in the picture! Website. Mr Chow is often featured in LA's DineLA week offering a chance to try a set menu at an affordable price.

11:30 am -- Walk to Teuscher Chocolates & Café

- Price: FREE
- Duration: 5 minutes

Walk up Camden Drive and turn right onto Brighton Way. Destination is on the corner.

11:35 am -- Teuscher Chocolates & Café

- Price: $5.00 (for a single adult)
- **Duration:** 15 minutes
- **Address:** 9548 Brighton Way, Beverly Hills, 90210

Teuscher (pronounced toy-sure) is considered one of the best chocolate makers in the world, if not the best according to National Geographic Traveler magazine.

The Champagne truffles - filled with infused Dom Perignon - are the first of its kind and are flown in from Switzerland every week especially! An 8oz box of 16 truffles will set you back $46 but definitely will make a once-in-a-lifetime gift for a family member or friend back home. They can be individually purchased and the staff are extremely friendly so don't feel bashful about doing so! Two Champagne truffles will cost about $6. If you are looking for a really unique gift, be sure to check their decorative boxes which come in fun characters. If you are on a budget, you can grab a hot chocolate or coffee from the cafe and sit outside and people watch. Website: www.teuscher-bh.com

11:50 am -- Walk to Martin Katz

- Price: FREE
- Duration: 5 minutes

Two doors down on the right towards Rodeo is Martin Katz.

11:55 am -- Martin Katz Ltd

- Price: FREE
- Duration: 5 minutes
- Address: 9540 Brighton Way, Beverly Hills, 90210

Take a peek in the window of world famous jeweler **Martin Katz**, known for mixing vintage styles and modern to create his unique designs desired by celebrities and their stylists especially at award season.

In 2008, he designed The Victoria's Secret Fantasy Bra valued at $5 million and set with 3,575 black diamonds, 117 1-carat white diamonds, 34 rubies, and 2 black diamond drops totaling 100 carats. More recently, he designed the world's first $1 million perfume bottle for DKNY's new Golden Delicious fragrance. The roll call of celebrities who like to wear his designs is like an Oscars party guest list and include Salma Hayek, Jennifer Aniston, Nicole Kidman, Angelina Jolie, Cate Blanchett, Kate Winslet, Jodie Foster, Jennifer Lopez and Heidi Klum.

12:00 pm -- Walk to Paley Center For Media

- **Price:** FREE
- **Duration:** 5 minutes

Continue up Brighton Way, cross over Rodeo Drive, turn left on N Beverly Drive. If you need to move your car due to parking time, you can now move it to the Paley Center for Media car park which is free.

12:05 pm -- Paley Center For Media

- **Price:** $10.00 (for a single adult)
- **Duration:** 1 hour
- **Address:** 465 N Beverly Dr Beverly Hills, CA 90210

Note: The center is closed Monday and Tuesdays. If you are doing your tour on this day, skip ahead to the next destination.

A research center for TV geeks and aficionados, **the Paley Center** also features cool TV themed exhibits - worth a visit whether you are a young fan or old. The exhibits change regularly - some recent highlights have been famous typewriters and props /costumes from TV shows, you can check out what's on, on their website or call them on 310 786 1091. Website: www.paleycenter.org

1:05 pm -- Travel to Nate N' Al's

- Price: FREE
- Duration: 5 minutes

Walk back down Beverly Drive. On the left hand side is **Nate N' Al's deli**.

1:10 pm -- Nate N' Al's Delicatessen

- **Price:** $15.00 (for a single adult)
- **Duration:** 45 minutes
- **Address:** 414 N Beverly Dr Beverly Hills, CA 90210

You'd never guess this modest little deli **Nate N' Al** - a hangout for Hollywood stars and agents. Local legend has it that Doris Day (who lived nearby on Crescent Drive for years) would stop by every day in her dressing gown for breakfast.

This Beverly Hills institution has been delivering up delicious sandwiches with their homemade rye bread is baked fresh daily, using a unique "double baked" process to make it crisp on the outside and soft on the inside, since 1945. Keep your eye out - you don't know who you may see. Regulars include Jon Voight, Larry King, Al Pacino and Lisa Kudrow and even the Kardashians! Local legend has it that Doris Day (who lived nearby on Crescent Drive for years) would stop by every day in her dressing gown for breakfast.

Their wide menu has something for every budget and taste bud. Highly recommended is the Nate N' Al Sandwich (pictured above) with its delicious Russian dressing and superb coleslaw.

Website: www.natenal.com

1:55 pm -- Walk to Beverly Hills Trolley

- Price: FREE
- Duration: 5 minutes

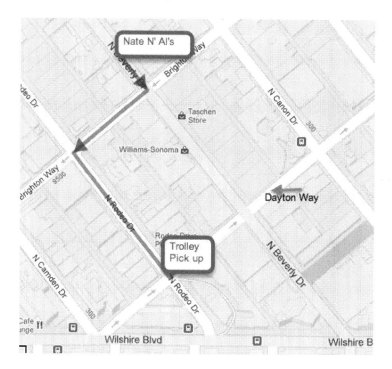

Walk down Beverly Drive, turn right on Brighton Way, then left onto Rodeo Drive. The Trolley stop is on the corner of Dayton Way and Rodeo Drive.

2:00 pm -- Beverly Hills Trolley Tours

- **Price:** $5.00 (for a single adult)
- **Duration:** 40 minutes
- **Address:** Dayton Way & Via Rodeo Dr Beverly Hills, CA 90212

Beverly Hills Trolley Tours operate Saturday and Sundays only in the winter, but Tuesdays thru Sundays in the summer (July to Sept). For an up-to-date schedule, check the website: www.beverlyhills.org

For just $5 per adult, $1 per child, this 40-minute tour will take you through some of Beverly Hills sights including celebrity homes, and architectural landmarks in the city including the infamous Witches House. Well worth the $5 and a fraction of the cost of other 'celebrity home' tours.

If the tour is not operating when you are doing your tour, skip ahead to the next destination.

2:40 pm -- Beverly Drive

- Price: FREE
- Duration: 5 minutes

Trace your steps back to Beverly Drive by walking back down Dayton Way towards Beverly Drive.

2:45 pm -- Shopping on Beverly Drive

- Price: $100.00 (for a single adult)
- Duration: 1 hour and 15 minutes
- Address: N Beverly Dr Beverly Hills, CA 90210

If you want to do some shopping so you can say you shopped in Beverly Hills, this is the place to do it with Gap, Crate & Barrel and other high street brands gracing this part of Beverly Hills. Beverly Drive and (the street parallel to it's right) Canon Drive are some of the more affordable places to shop in Beverly Hills.

Pop into **The Cheese Store of Beverly Hills** (opposite **Nate N' Al's**) and try a few free samples, and pick up a Cheese 101 DVD as a gift for someone back home. **Website:** www.cheesestorebh.com

Another great gift for someone back home is some chocolate from **Edelweiss Chocolates** (444 N Cannon Drive) - handmade in Beverly Hills, this chocolate shop has fixed the sweet tooth of Katherine Hepburn, Frank Sinatra and Oprah among many others! **Website:** www.edelweisschocolates.com

The Beverly Hills Visitors Bureau sells gifts with the infamous Beverly Hills Shield on, if you are looking for a memento of your visit. **Website:** www.lovebeverlyhills.org

If you get tired from shopping, you can stop for a coffee from **Starbucks** or **The Coffee Bean & Tea Leaf**, (California's answer to Starbucks with excellent teas), at the top of Beverly Drive (near the **Paley Center**). Be sure to wear dark shades to hide your gawking eyes as you try to celeb spot!

4:00 pm -- Walk to Sprinkles Cupcakes

- **Price:** FREE
- **Duration:** 10 minutes

Photo from the Sugafina Facebook page.

Depending on where you are on Beverly Blvd, walk up to Santa Monica Blvd and then left on Santa Monica towards N Camden Drive. Before you reach the next stop pop into **Sugarfina** a gourmet candy shop offering gummies, chocolate, caramels and more from around the world, it's just on the right hand side of the street if you are coming up from Rodeo or N Beverly. A box of Champagne gummy bears makes a great gift for a friend... or you. We won't judge.

If you prefer your gifts to last longer there's also the **Only In Beverly Hills** store selling all sorts of items from totes to baseball caps. The OIBH store is also on the right side of the street just a few doors before **Sprinkles**. **Website:** www.onlyinbeverlyhills.com

4:10 pm -- Sprinkles Cupcakes

- Price: $3.50 (for a single adult)
- Duration: 20 minutes
- Address: 9635 S Santa Monica Blvd Beverly Hills, CA 90212

After all that shopping you need something sweet like a cupcake or ice cream cone and where better than **Sprinkles** - considered to be the World's first cupcake bakery, and home to the cupcake ATM. Inspired by a 2002trip to NY to visit her sister, Candace Nelson and her husband Charles set out on a 2-year venture to create the perfect cupcake. Once they created their perfect cupcake, they took a big risk and opened this store. They need not have worried because on that first day, the cupcakes sold out in three hours, and within the first week 2,000 cupcakes were sold!

Sprinkles has grown to 10 locations throughout the United States and now sells delicious ice cream, cookies and cupcakes for your dog as well. Not to worry if the store is closed as you can use the World's first Cupcake ATM, which is open 24 hours! Follow them on Twitter to get the secret password of the day and score some free treats: https://twitter.com/sprinklesbh

Recommended is the Red Velvet cupcake and we are big fans of the delicious ice cream next door!

Website: www.sprinkles.com

Watching your calories? Try **Go Greek Yogurt** just around the corner on Bedford Drive or **Pressed Juicery** just past Go Greek.

4:30 pm -- Walk to Beverly Hills Shield

- Price: FREE
- Duration: 10 minutes

If you want your picture taken with the iconic **Beverly Hills shield** and to walk off that cupcake, you can take the 10 minute walk down Santa Monica Blvd (southwesterly) towards Wilshire Blvd. Cross over Wilshire Blvd and on the corner of Santa Monica and Moreno Drive, next to Sonya Dakar skin clinic, you will find one of the iconic shields!

If not, skip to the next destination.

4:40 pm -- Walk to The Luxe Hotel

- Price: FREE
- Duration: 20 minutes

Walk back down Santa Monica Blvd to Rodeo Drive. Turn right on Rodeo Drive, cross over Brighton Way. Your destination is on the left hand side of the road.

5:00 pm -- The Luxe Hotel

- **Price:** $15.00 (for a single adult)
- **Duration:** 1 hour
- **Address:** 360 N. Rodeo Dr. Los Angeles, California 90210

Photo from the Luxe Hotel Facebook.

Possibly one of the cheapest happy hours at **Luxe** the only hotel on Rodeo Drive itself. From 4pm to 7pm, well cocktails are $6 with beer at $4.

6:00 pm -- Dinner and drinks

- **Price:** $50.00 (for a single adult)
- **Duration:** 5 hours
- **Address:** Beverly Hills, California 90210

Photo from the Love Beverly Hills Facebook page.

Beverly Hills has many restaurants, particularly Italian. Reservations are recommended for most Beverly Hills restaurants. All restaurants mentioned are within walking distance.

Insider Tip: **DineLA** *where many top restaurants do a fixed price menu for a week is a great opportunity to try the more pricey restaurants of Beverly Hills on more affordable way. The DineLA dates change so see website for details: www.dinela.com*

Mulbery Street Pizza
Address: 240 S Beverly Drive, Beverly Hills.
Price:$.
Website: http://mulberrypizzeria.com
What They're Known For: Thin crust New York style pizza that celebrities and every day folk adore!

The Cheesecake Factory
Address: 364 N Beverly Dr, Beverly Hills
Price $$.
Website: www.cheesecakefactory.com
What They're Known For: This is the original location. Generous portions and an enormous menu with so much choice it will make your head spin.

M Cafe
Address: 9433 Brighton Way, Beverly Hills.
Price $$.
Website: www.mcafedechaya.com
What They're Known For: Macrobiotic and Vegan food that can be enjoyed by everyone! The Peanut Kale salad is a local favorite!

Il Fornaio Cucina Italiana
Address: 301 N.Beverly Drive, Beverly Hills.
Price $$.
Website: www.ilfornaio.com
What They're Known For: Fantastic Italian food and homemade bread.

La Scala

Address: 434 N Canon Drive, Beverly Hills

Price: $$.

Website: www.lascalabeverlyhills.com

What They're Known For: Keeping it old school with their chopped salads. Marilyn Monroe had her last meal sent from here on the night she died. Elizabeth Taylor got meals delivered when she was filming Cleopatra and the words to Moon River were written here.

If you want to splash out on a very expensive dinner, you have plenty of choices! Reservations are a must. Some suggestions include:

Cut

Address: Beverly Wilshire Hotel, 9500 Wilshire Blvd, Beverly Hills.

Price $$$$.

Website: www.wolfgangpuck.com

What They're Known For: Wolfgang Puck's steakhouse inside the Beverly Wilshire Hotel. Used to be a firm favorite for Tom Cruise and Katie Holmes.

Spago

Address: 176 N Canon Dr, Beverly Hills.

Price $$$$.

Website: http://www.wolfgangpuck.com

What They're Known For: Wolfgang Puck's flagship Spago is new American cuisine - if you are lucky, you may meet the man himself. Reverse happy hour from 9 pm - 11 pm on drinks!

SugarFish by Sushi Nozawa

Address: 212 N Canon Dr, Beverly Hills.
Price: $$$$.
Website: www.sugarfishsushi.com
What They're Known For: No reservations high-end sushi bar - you will not find any California Rolls here.

Maude

Address: 212 S Beverly Dr, Beverly Hills.
Price: $$$$.
Website: www.mauderestaurant.com
What They're Known For: Voted one of LA's Best New Restaurants of 2014 Chef Curtis Stone's restaurant serves up tasting menus centered around one flavor each month eg: June is Avocados. Reservations only.

Alternatively take a taxi/car sharing service back to the start of the tour:

Polo Lounge

Address: Beverly Hills Hotel, 9641 Sunset Boulevard, Beverly Hills
Price $$$$.
Website: www.dorchestercollection.com
What They're Known For: Fine dining in a historic hotel. Maybe you'll spot someone! Recommended: Rib Eye Steak or the chopped salad.

After dinner drinks

Vampire Lounge
Address: 9865 Santa Monica Blvd, Beverly Hills.
Price: $$.
Website: www.vampiretastingroom.com
What They're Known For: Cozy atmosphere and delicious wine from the Vampire Winery that Dracula would be happy with.

Bar Noir
Address: Maison 140 Hotel,140 S Lasky Dr, Beverly Hills.
Price: $$.
Website: www.maison140.com
What They're Known For: The antique absinthe fountain at the end of the bar and absinthe happy hour (5 pm - 7 pm).

Nic's Beverly Hills
Address: 453 N Canon Dr, Beverly Hills.
Price: $$$.
Website: www.nicsbeverlyhills.com
What They're Known For: Vodbox (vodka freezer room) they provide the coats and amazing oysters. Happy Hour 4-7pm. Live music and DJs some nights and door fee - see website.

Evening Activities

If you have the time and are driving its worth a quick drive or walk up and down Rodeo Drive at night as the shops are quite amazing looking after dark.

Also worth a look is the **Electric Fountain** at the intersection of Wilshire and Santa Monica Boulevards with its changing colored lights and water jets - it was the first of its kind when it was built in 1931. You may recall it from the quintessential Beverly Hills movie Clueless.

Check what's on at **The Wallis** bring world-class theater, dance, and music to Beverly Hills: www.thewallis.org

The Academy (yes the same one that presents the Oscars) hold numerous screenings that the public can attend throughout the year check their website for details: www.oscars.org/events

The **Beverly Hills Laemmle** shows movies and often has Q&A with directors and actors. See website: www.laemmle.com

The gorgeous Art Deco theater **The Saban Theatre** has concerts, movies, and performances. See website for schedule: www.sabanconcerts.com

Throughout the year **The City of Beverly Hills** puts on numerous events from movie nights, to free concerts and car shows for details see website: www.lovebeverlyhills.org

Things You Need to Know (Appendix)

"You know, you're really nobody in LA unless you live in a house with a really big door. " - Steve Martin

The tour is designed to be done by foot and its approximately 2 miles and it's easy for every ability, and age.

Mix It Up - This tour can also be done from lunch to late evening. Rodeo Drive is safe at night and particularly spectacular during Christmas time with lots of lights. If you choose to do this, please note Paley Center and Beverly Hills Trolley tours close early.

Parking - Beverly Hills is full of free parking during the day but the lots get expensive at night. You can usually find metered street parking on one of the side streets so carry quarters or a credit card for those. See website: www.beverlyhills.org

What to Wear - While the rule of Los Angeles is to treat everyone as if they are someone, no matter how they are dressed, because they could be someone - known as the Pretty Woman rule, you will probably feel more comfortable dressed smart casual at night especially in some of the higher end restaurants. Daytime - anything goes but if you want to blend in and not look like a tourist, don the celebrities favorite incognito look - dark shades and the baseball hat. If you are desperate to see a celeb, go during the week as you are much less likely to on weekends, and look for the paparazzi - if they are waiting outside somewhere, the likelihood is someone important is inside!

Taxis - Taxis are very hard to hail on the street, so be sure to either get a hotel to hail you one or book online; you can also find various smartphone apps to hail a taxi like Curbed. For taxis during evening activities like drinking and eating, consider ride sharing services like Lyft, and Uber. If you are using any of these services for the first time, use these discount coupon codes:

- For Uber coupon use: UBERSELFGUIDETOLA
- For Lyft coupon use: CLARE758131

Public Transport - Depending on where you are staying, you could take public transport to The Beverly Hills Hotel but you would have to walk (25 mins) to the next stop. You can also take it just to Rodeo Drive. For details about riding LA transit and tickets please see the Metro website which has a trip planner, maps to download for offline use, an app and Next Trip so you can find out when the next bus is due. An all day pass costs $7. Website: www.metro.net

Evening Activities - It's worth checking out sites like Groupon, LivingSocial, and GoldStar before you visit to see what is happening and whether you can get discounted tickets.

Some myths about Los Angeles:

- It's always sunny. Los Angeles has about 15 inches of rain a year. In May, we have May Gray and in June, we have June Gloom where it's overcast virtually every day. Best months for weather are September and October where it's normally sunny and hot around 75F.
- "No one walks in LA" as The Missing Persons sang in the 80s. Well, times have changed and although LA is spread out, many areas of the city have become pedestrian friendly and there is a very active and successful movement to encourage getting Angelinos out of their cars and walking and cycling instead.
- Traffic is terrible. With 26 million cars in the city, I'd be lying if I said we have no traffic. And it's true that we do refer to places as the time it takes to get to, not the miles and LA's traffic is 2nd worst in the country (sorry DC) but as long as you avoid rush hour, 8-10am and 4pm-7pm, you'll be fine.
- Everyone works in showbiz. Actually, our number one industry is manufacturing and we are the largest manufacturing center in the US!

- Everyone is image conscious, only in certain areas like you would get in other major cities like New York, London, or Paris. One of the nice things about LA is most service people know to treat everyone as if they are someone, no matter how they are dressed, because they could be someone - known as the Pretty Woman rule.
- It's full of gangs and is dangerous. Actually, LA's crime rate has been dropping consistently for the last 10 years. However, you should still take the same precautions you would in any major city - keep an eye on your valuables, especially smartphones, don't flash wads of cash, and don't leave valuables exposed in locked cars.

Additional websites for information:

- Official City of Beverly Hills: www.beverlyhills.org
- Beverly Hills Tourism site: www.lovebeverlyhills.com

About the Author

FEEDBACK AND MORE INFORMATION:

If you have questions or feedback on this tour please feel free to contact me at restouristLA@gmail.com

You can also follow me on Twitter @ResTourist or Instagram @ResidentTouristLA or Facebook https://www.facebook.com/selfguidetoLA

See the rest of my Southern California tours available on Amazon: http://tinyurl.com/LAselfguide or through Unanchor: http://www.unanchor.com/user/clareauchterlonie

Clare Auchterlonie

Since 2001 I have lived in Los Angeles, I came here on a whim from London and for the most part I haven't looked back. Maybe once, when I ran out of tea bags. Always looking for new things to discover in my adopted city – I'm a Resident Tourist!

Twitter: @restourist

Blog: http://www.facebook.com/selfguidetoLA

Unanchor

Chief Itinerary Coordinator

Unanchor wants your opinion

Your next travel adventure starts now. A simple review on Amazon will grant you and a travel buddy, friend, or human of your choosing any of the wonderful Unanchor digital itineraries for free.

What a deal!

Leave a review:

- http://www.amazon.com/unanchor

Collect your guides

- Send an email to reviews@unanchor.com with a link to your review.

- Wait with bated breath.

- Receive your new travel adventure in your inbox!

Other Unanchor Itineraries

Africa

- One Day in Africa - A Guide to Tangier
- Johannesburg/Pretoria: A 4-Day South Africa Tour Itinerary
- Cape Town - What not to miss on a 4-day first-timers' itinerary

Asia

China

- Beijing Must Sees, Must Dos, Must Eats - 3-Day Tour Itinerary
- Shanghai 3-Day Tour Itinerary
- 2 Days in Shanghai: A Budget-Conscious Peek at Modern China

India

- 3-Day Budget Delhi Itinerary
- Delhi in 3 Days - A Journey Through Time
- 3 Days Highlights of Mumbai
- A 3-Day Tryst with 300-Year-Old Kolkata
- Kolkata (Calcutta): 2 Days of Highlights

Japan

- Nozawa Onsen's Winter Secrets - A 3-Day Tour
- 3-Day Highlights of Tokyo
- Tour Narita During an Airport Layover

Singapore

- The Affordable Side of Singapore: A 4-Day Itinerary
- A First Timer's Guide to 3 Days in the City that Barely Sleeps - Singapore
- Singapore: 3 Fun-Filled Days on this Tiny Island
- Family Friendly Singapore - 3 Days in the Lion City

Rest of Asia

- Between the Skyscrapers - Hong Kong 3-Day Discovery Tour
- Art and Culture in Ubud, Bali – 1-Day Highlights
- Go with the Sun to Borobudur & Prambanan in 1 Day
- 3 Days in the Vibrant City of Seoul and the Serene Countryside of Gapyeong
- A 3-Day Thrilla in Manila then Flee to the Sea
- Manila on a Budget: 2-Day Itinerary
- The Very Best of Moscow in 3 Days
- Saint Petersburg in Three Days
- The Two Worlds of Kaohsiung in 5 Days
- 72 Hours in Taipei: The All-rounder
- Girls' Weekend in Bangkok: Shop, Spa, Savour, Swoon
- The Ins and Outs of Bangkok: A 3-Day Guide
- Saigon 3-Day Beyond the Guidebook Itinerary

Central America
Mexico

- Your Chiapas Adventure: San Cristobal de las Casas and Palenque, Mexico 5-Day Itinerary (2nd Edition)
- Everything to see or do in Mexico City - 7-Day Itinerary
- Todo lo que hay que ver o hacer en la Ciudad de México - Itinerario de 7 Días
- Mexico City 3-Day Highlights Itinerary
- Cancun and Mayan Riviera 5-Day Itinerary (4th Edition)

Europe
France
Paris

- Paris to Chartres Cathedral: 1-Day Tour Itinerary
- Discover Mont St Michel: 2-Night Stay
- Paris 3-Day Walking Tour: See Paris Like a Local
- Paris for Free: 3 Days
- Art Lovers' Paris: A 2-Day Artistic Tour of the City of Lights
- Paris 4-Day Winter Wonderland
- The Best of Paris in One Day
- Paris Foodie Classics: 1 Day of French Food
- Paris 1-Day Itinerary - Streets of Montmartre

Greece

- Athens 3-Day Highlights Tour Itinerary
- Chania & Sfakia, Greece & Great Day Trips Nearby (5-Day Itinerary)
- 2-Day Beach Tour: Travel like a Local in Sithonia Peninsula, Halkidiki, Greece
- Thessaloniki, Greece - 3-Day Highlights Itinerary
- Day Trip From Thessaloniki to Kassandra Peninsula, Halkidiki, Greece

Italy

- A 3-Day Tour Around Ancient Rome
- 3 Days of Roman Adventure: spending time and money efficiently in Rome
- Discover Rome's Layers: A 3-Day Walking Tour
- A Day on Lake Como, Italy
- Milan Unknown - A 3-day tour itinerary
- Landscape, Food, & Trulli: 1 Week in Puglia, the Valle d'Itria, and Matera
- 3-Day Florence Walking Tours
- Florence, Italy 3-Day Art & Culture Itinerary
- See Siena in a Day
- Three Romantic Walks in Venice

Netherlands

- Amsterdam 3-Day Alternative Tour: Not just the Red Light District
- Amsterdam Made Easy: A 3-Day Guide
- Two-day tour of Utrecht: the smaller, less touristy Amsterdam!

Spain

- Mijas - One Day Tour of an Andalucían White Village
- Málaga, Spain – 2-Day Tour from the Moors to Picasso
- Two-Day Tour in Sunny Seville, Spain
- FC Barcelona: More than a Club (A 1-Day Experience)
- 3-Day Highlights of Barcelona Itinerary
- Ibiza on a Budget - Three-Day Itinerary
- Three days exploring Logroño and La Rioja by public transport
- Best of Valencia 2-Day Guide

United Kingdom

England

London

- London's Historic City Wall Walk (1-2 days)
- London 1-Day Literary Highlights
- The 007 James Bond Day Tour of London
- An Insider's Guide to the Best of London in 3 Days
- Done London? A 3-day itinerary for off the beaten track North Norfolk
- London's South Bank - Off the Beaten Track 1-Day Tour
- London for Free :: Three-Day Tour
- Low-Cost, Luxury London - 3-Day Itinerary
- London's Villages - A 3-day itinerary exploring Hampstead, Marylebone and Notting Hill
- 3-Day London Tour for Olympic Visitors

Rest of England

- Bath: An Exploring Guide - 2-Day Itinerary
- 2-Day Brighton Best-of Walks & Activities
- Bristol in 2 Days: A Local's Guide
- MADchester - A Local's 3-Day Guide To Manchester
- One Day in Margate, UK on a Budget

Rest of United Kingdom

- History, Culture, and Craic: 3 Days in Belfast, Ireland
- The Best of Edinburgh: A 3-Day Journey from Tourist to Local
- Two-Day Self-Guided Walks - Cardiff

Rest of Europe

- 3 Days in Brussels - The grand sites via the path less trodden
- Zagreb For Art Lovers: A Three-Day Itinerary
- 3-Day Prague Beer Pilgrimage
- Best of Prague - 3-Day Itinerary
- 3 Days in Helsinki
- Weekend Break: Tbilisi - Crown Jewel of the Caucasus
- A 3-Day Guide to Berlin, Germany
- 2 Days In Berlin On A Budget
- 3 Days in Dublin City - City Highlights, While Eating & Drinking Like a Local
- Krakow: Three-Day Tour of Poland's Cultural Capital
- Best of Warsaw 2-Day Itinerary
- Lisbon in 3 Days: Budget Itinerary
- Braşov - Feel the Pulse of Transylvania in 3 Days
- Lausanne 1-Day Tour Itinerary

Middle East

- Amman 2-Day Cultural Tour
- Adventure Around Amman: A 2-Day Itinerary
- 3 Days as an Istanbulite: An Istanbul Itinerary
- Between the East and the West, a 3-Day Istanbul Itinerary

North America

Canada

- Relax in Halifax for Two Days Like a Local
- An Insider's Guide to Toronto: Explore the City Less Traveled in Three Days
- Toronto: A Multicultural Retreat (3-day itinerary)
- The Best of Toronto - 2-Day Itinerary

United States

California

Los Angeles

- 2-Day Los Angeles Vegan and Vegetarian Foodie Itinerary
- Downtown Los Angeles 1-Day Walking Tour
- Sunset Strip, Los Angeles - 1-Day Walking Tour
- Los Angeles Highlights 3-Day Itinerary
- Hollywood, Los Angeles - 1-Day Walking Tour
- Los Angeles On A Budget - 4-Day Tour Itinerary
- Los Angeles 4-Day Itinerary (partly using Red Tour Bus)

San Francisco

- San Francisco 2-Day Highlights Itinerary
- The Tech Lover's 48-Hour Travel Guide to Silicon Valley & San Francisco
- San Francisco Foodie Weekend Itinerary

Rest of California

- Orange County 3-Day Budget Itinerary
- Beverly Hills, Los Angeles - 1-Day Tour
- Wine, Food, and Fun: 3 Days in Napa Valley
- Beyond the Vine: 2-Day Napa Tour
- Palm Springs, Joshua Tree & Salton Sea: A 3-Day Itinerary
- Beer Lovers 3-Day Guide To Northern California
- RVA Haunts, History, and Hospitality: Three Days in Richmond, Virginia
- Best of the Best: Three-Day San Diego Itinerary

- Three Days in Central California's Wine Country

Florida

- 2 Days Exploring Haunted Key West
- 3-Day Discover Orlando Itinerary
- Three Days in the Sunshine City of St. Petersburg, Florida

Hawaii

- Lesser-known Oahu in 4 Days on a Budget
- Local's Guide to Oahu - 3-Day Tour Itinerary
- Tackling 10 Must-Dos on the Big Island in 3 Days

Illinois

- 3-Day Chicago Highlights Itinerary
- 6-Hour "Layover" Chicago
- Famous Art & Outstanding Restaurants in Chicago 1-Day Itinerary
- Chicago Food, Art and Funky Neighborhoods in 3 Days

Kansas

- The Best of Kansas City: 3-Day Itinerary
- Day Trek Along the Hudson River
- Wichita From Cowtown to Air Capital in 2 Days

Massachusetts

- Navigating Centuries of Boston's Nautical History in One Day
- Rainy Day Boston One-Day Itinerary
- Boston 2-Day Historic Highlights Itinerary

New York

- Brooklyn, NY 2-Day Foodie Tour
- A Local's Guide to Montauk, New York in 2 Days - From the Ocean to the Hills
- Day Trip from New York City: Mountains, Falls, & a Funky Town
- Weekend Day Trip from New York City: The Wine & Whiskey Trail
- New York Like A Native: Five Boroughs in Six Days
- New York City - First Timer's 2-Day Walking Tour
- 3-Day Amazing Asian Food Tour of New York City!
- New York City's Lower East Side, 1-Day Tour Itinerary
- Hidden Bars of New York City's East Village & Lower East Side: A 2-Evening Itinerary
- Jewish New York in Two Days
- Lower Key, Lower Cost: Lower Manhattan - 1-Day Itinerary
- Weekend Tour of Portland's Craft Breweries, Wineries, & Distilleries
- Day Trip from New York City: Heights of the Hudson Valley (Bridges and Ridges)

Pennsylvania

- A Laid-Back Long Weekend in Austin, TX
- 3 Day PA Dutch Country Highlights (Lancaster County, PA)
- Two Days in Philadelphia
- Pittsburgh: Three Days Off the Beaten Path

Rest of United States

- Alaska Starts Here - 3 Days in Seward
- The Best of Phoenix & Scottsdale: 3-Day Itinerary
- Tucson: 3 Days at the Intersection of Mexico, Native America & the Old West
- The Best of Boulder, CO: A Three-Day Guide
- Louisville: Three Days in Derby City
- A Local's Guide to the Hamptons 3 Day Itinerary
- New Haven Highlights: Art, Culture & History 3-Day Itinerary
- Atlanta 3-Day Highlights
- Savannah 3-Day Highlights Itinerary
- La Grange, Kentucky: A 3-Day Tour Itinerary
- New Orleans 3-Day Itinerary
- Baltimore: A Harbor, Parks, History, Seafood & Art - 3-Day Itinerary
- Summer in Jackson Hole: Local Tips for the Perfect Three to Five Day Adventure
- Las Vegas on a Budget - 3-Day Itinerary
- Las Vegas - Gaming Destination Diversions - Ultimate 3-Day Itinerary
- Cruisin' Asbury like a Local in 1 Day
- Girls' 3-Day Weekend Summer Getaway in Asheville, NC
- Five Days in the Wild Outer Banks of North Carolina
- Family Weekend in Columbus, OH
- Ohio State Game Day Weekend
- Portland Bike and Bite: A 2-Day Itinerary
- Three Days Livin' as a True and Local Portlander
- Corpus Christi: The Insider Guide for a 4-Day Tour
- An Active 2-3 Days In Moab, Utah
- The Weekenders Guide To Burlington, Vermont
- Washington, DC in 4 Days
- Washington, DC: 3 Days Like a Local
- A Day on Bainbridge Island

Oceania
Australia

- Two Wheels and Pair of Cozzies: the Best of Newcastle in 3 Days
- A Weekend Snapshot of Sydney
- Sydney, Australia - 3-Day **Best Of** Itinerary
- The Blue Mountains: A weekend of nature, culture and history.
- Laneway Melbourne: A One-Day Walking Tour
- Magic of Melbourne 3-Day Tour
- A Weekend Snapshot of Melbourne
- An Afternoon & Evening in Melbourne's Best Hidden Bars
- Best of Perth's Most Beautiful Sights in 3 Days

New Zealand

- Enjoy the Rebuild - Christchurch 2-Day Tour
- The Best of Wellington: 3-Day Itinerary

South America
Argentina

- Buenos Aires Best Kept Secrets: 2-Day Itinerary
- An Insider's Guide to the Best of Buenos Aires in 3 Days
- 2-Day Tour Around Salta, the Pretty One

Peru

- Arequipa - A 2-Day Itinerary for First-Time Visitors
- A 1-Day Foodie's Dream Tour of Arequipa
- Cusco and the Sacred Valley - a five-day itinerary for a first-time visitor
- Little Known Lima 3-Day Tour

Rest of South America

- Sights & Sounds of São Paulo - 3-Day Itinerary

Unanchor is a global family for travellers to experience the world with the heart of a local.

UNANCHOR

Made in the USA
Middletown, DE
06 March 2019